THE MAIN CAUSES OF MORAL EROSION AND INDISCIPLINE IN NIGERIA

HADI ABDULLAHI ALKANCHI

ISBN: 9798353453260

DEDICATION

To my family

CONTENTS

INTRODUCTION

Glory be to Allah, the Magnificent and the merciful. It was in His infinite wisdom that He taught man how to write with pen and also taught him what he didn't know. May the mercy of Allah also be upon His devout servant and messenger Prophet Mohammed (peace be upon him), his entire family, his companions and all his followers whose various contributions to Islam help sustain the light of Islam perpetually.

Besides, the writing of this booklet has proved to be a very difficult task for me though not surprising considering the fact I am still a learner myself. The completion of this book was made possible by the guidance of Allah and the sincere intentions of the writer.

The main purpose of this book is to call the attention of all the citizens of this great nation to the social vices that have been afflicting our country for a long period of years. It is also the intention of this humble book to suggest practical strategies that will emancipate this country from these social vices that have inevitably rendered the Nigerian community, into all-around special confusion.

Some readers of this book may think or suppose certain statements, or groups of people are advertently over-repeated, but this situation is not intended. All the repetitions X are intended to bring to light certain behavioural qualities entitled "pillars of character and discipline", and certain groups of people whose primary social responsibility is to inculcate character and discipline in the citizens of this nation. Namely, these groups are:

- Parents,
- Teachers,
- Leaders,
- Mass Media,
- Businessmen and women.

These social groups and the pillars of characters and discipline are the basis of this book. Therefore, except for the last chapter of this book, all the chapters enunciate these two aspects. On the other hand, in the last chapter, I pointed out the practical strategies that eradicate social, economic and religious indiscipline in Nigeria.

CHAPTER ONE

MAIN SOURCES OF MORAL STANDARDS AND DISCIPLINE IN NIGERIA

Abu Sa'id El Khadiri, may Allah be pleased with him, once said "*I heard Prophet Mohammed (peace and blessing of Allah be upon him) saying, if any of you comes across an evil, he should try to stop it with hand (using force). If he is not in a position to stop it with his hand then he should try to stop it utilizing his tongue (meaning he should speak against it). If he is not even able to use his tongue then he should at least condemn it in his heart. This is the weakest degree of faith*".

This Hadith is urging every Muslim to abstain from unlawful acts and also preach against the commission of such acts by other Muslims, this implies that a Muslim should not assume attitudes of indifference about situations on events surrounding him/her. Every Muslim should utilise whatever is at his disposal, knowledge, power, wealth etc. to fight against any form of blasphemy and indiscipline. Lack of character training and general etiquette is contrary to Islamic Principles and Laws. Consequently, it is incumbent upon every Muslim to strive hard to see the success of the current war against indiscipline in Nigeria.

Character training is variously defined by different cultures. In Hausa culture, character training is the art of building or socializing the young ones to learn and adopt the norms and values of their community to ensure their acceptable membership.
On the other hand, general etiquette, in Hausa culture means abiding by the formal rules and regulations governing the day-to-day social interactions among the members of the community. A person who can cultivate these qualities is considered well-bred.

A well-bred person is distinguishable by certain human qualities. These qualities are pre-requisite for a sound moral character and general etiquette. These qualities are:

- Faith
- Modesty
- patience
- Self-Control
- Patriotism
- Honesty and Trust Worthiness.

In a community where its members fail to achieve these qualities, that community will be infected with social problems such as indiscipline, corruption, theft, anarchy and moral decadence.

As earlier mentioned character training differs from culture to culture. Some simple examples will buttress this fact. In the Hausa Community, it is a responsibility for every married person or adult to cease frequenting such public places as Cinema houses, Beer-parlous, Night clubs etc. This is to avoid the embarrassment of bumping into relatives, particularly the youth, moreover, when married one is expected to spend one's time, especially the night hours with one’s immediate family. To do otherwise is a breach of one's responsibilities. But in European cultures, age or marital responsibilities is not a hindrance to attending public places.

The upbringing of a child in the Hausa community is accomplished through communal efforts. The parents of the child are as responsible for the upbringing of the child as their neighbours are. The neighbours are expected and encouraged to contribute to the disciplining of the child as well as in other aspects of child socialization. Again in European cultures, it is the prerogative of only the immediate family to upbringing their child. It is the immediate family apart from school that is responsible for its young ones.

The communal efforts and equality of members in the Hausa community are also injected into its educational system for the young. In local schools where the children learn about Islam and secular knowledge, all the children in the community are taught together under the instruction of one Mallam (Teacher), children from the rich, the poor or the ruling class are treated equally and receive the same instruction. Contrary to this, Western education allows for separate schools (Private schools) for the wealthy, while children from poor families languish in under-equipped schools.

Sometimes they even have to go with no education at all.

The preceding examples show us that although culture is universal it differs from society to society. Similarly, the modes of character, training and discipline differ from one society to another. Therefore Nigerians must cherish their cultural heritage and expatiate on these cultural aspects which they share with other cultures to enhance inter cultural understanding.

THE ORIGINATORS OF THE MORAL STANDARDS AND INDISCIPLINE IN NIGERIA

In Nigerian society there are certain categories of people who are assigned the responsibilities of socializing with other members of the society so that they can achieve good character, to enable them to survive and contribute to their society. These categories of special people are as follows:-

- Parents
- Teachers
- Leaders
- Mass media
- Businessmen and Women
- General public.

To inculcate discipline, moral character and hard work in Nigeria, every category of these people must work extra hard using the Hadith mentioned on the first page as a guideline to fight against social vices. But these people must be exemplary themselves.

Nowadays, in Nigerian society, the leaders share the greatest fraction of the blame for the lack of discipline moral decadence and total disregard for culture. Excess drinking, chasing women, indiscipline, and extravagance are just a few vices committed by most of our leaders. These and other vices are the vogues in Nigeria.

Parents, well-disciplined and ideal households are quite a few in Nigeria today. The sole cause of this quandary is the parents who are unreasonably permissive with their children. For most parents, their desire to acquire wealth overrides their obligations to their children. They don't have time to interact with and know more about their children. Other parents on the other hand are always absent from home. They indulge themselves in extramarital activities such as drinking, adultery, gambling etc.

Religious leaders are also to blame. The religious leaders are very active in the current frenzy to acquire wealth. Some of them preach purposely to acquire wealth. Some do it to intimidate or incite one group of people against another. Only a few of them are true preachers.

The teacher of 'Western Education' is also in this. The greatest indiscipline of these teachers is the habit of befriending their students, in the negative sense, that a good number of teachers turn their highly respected cloak of teaching and expose their nakedness. Some are not even ashamed to be seen publicly with their students-girl friends. Another disgracing group of a teacher is the drunken teachers. They are drunk day-in-and-day-out their favourite hobby is to come to their classrooms tipsy and make a mockery of themselves and the teaching profession.

The wealthy are the forces of erosion that eat away the foundation of moral characters, patriotism, nationalism and dedication in our society. They are hoarders, smugglers, bribery givers, extravagant, arrogant and most ostentatious. To instil discipline in our country Nigeria, tip holds our characters and culture, we shall pull our strength together and use the Hadith as our guiding force and fight against the menace in our society today. Every member of society, the readers, the authors, our teachers, leaders, parents, the well-to-do, the poor, etc. must all contribute both in deed speech, and materials. To accomplish this task is very easy if we can allow ourselves to be observed by the spirit of the war against indiscipline. But all must work interdependently. War against indiscipline can only succeed if we give it a chance.

Let us all struggle hard to acquire the five qualities discussed earlier on. For this, if the war against indiscipline is pursued to the total eradication of indiscipline lack of morals and other social vices,

Nigeria stands to reap large profits that can sustain her perpetually. Some of the advantages (Profits) are as follows:

- ❖ Unity, peace and Good life
- ❖ Discipline
- ❖ Ability to shun Temptation, Corruption and Materialism.
- ❖ Justice
- ❖ Incorruptible leaders.

Justice is very crucial in any society, it is the pillar that holds any society from falling into total anarchy. It also installs confidence in the hearts of the members of the society in their leaders. Leaders in our Nigerian society must give heed to a legal system that is impartial, uniform and effective. Every defaulter must be brought to book and a fair trial must be ensured.

Here are a few suggestions:

- ❖ Every citizen must be law-abiding;
- ❖ All offences must be punishable and offenders must be penalised accordingly;
- ❖ No differential penalties for the well-placed and the poor;
- ❖ All criminal public servants must be publicly probed and punished/acquitted accordingly;
- ❖ Idolised teachers and uplift the condition of service for them.

Finally, I will conclude this sermon by praying to

Allah to make war against indiscipline (WAI) a success and also aid its champions in their crusade. I also pray to Allah to enable us to practice the teachings of war against indiscipline in all aspects of our lives.

CHAPTER TWO

MAIN CAUSE OF MORAL EROSION AND INDISCIPLINE IN NIGERIA

The main cause of moral erosion and indiscipline in Nigeria is the deplorable attitude of indifference to some vital human virtues by the Inhabitants of this country. These virtues are as follows:

- Faith,
- Modesty,
- Patience,
- Uprightness (Honesty).

These virtues prevailed in this country in the good old days. In those days Nigeria reached its zenith because its social and human structures were based on these virtues. Unfortunately, nowadays many undesirable virtues of a foreign land are infiltrating into this land sweeping away all the human and social structures in their way and imposing an unreliable framework of materialism to which people naively succumb.

In those days people adaptably related to each other through these virtues, hence the virtues were accorded with prestige their possessor the highest honour. Unfortunately, now the secular framework of materialism has brutally replaced all that.

This new life of possessions and ostentation leads its champions and disciples astray. Our leaders should understand this and decisively intervene to save the situation before it is too late. May Allah show us the right path Amen.

WEAK FAITH

The inhabitants of Nigeria particularly the Muslims are currently engaged in vices that will ultimately diminish their faith and render them completely valuable to various temptations.

In Islam faith or a faithful person is one who wholeheartedly believes in Allah, his angels, the divine books, all the prophets and the "*Day of Judgment*". Also, he should believe in predestination, whether good or bad they are all from Allah.

The exponent of a Muslim's faith is a total commitment to Trust Worthiness, truthfulness, righteousness, and respect for human rights. Some common characteristics of faith are, total abstinence from; blasphemy, drinking, gambling, adultery/fornication etc. Therefore it is our lawful duty as Muslims to strive hard to acquire these qualities to obtain with the blessings of our creator (Allah).

Obedience to Allah and abiding by his decrees had been advocated by all the divine religions. Therefore the cultivation of the earlier outlined virtues is a task that must be done by all the inhabitants of this country, not just the Muslims. Many people in Nigeria have lost these qualities so they lack moral standards and general discipline. And this is caused by weak faith.

Indiscipline and other social vices in Nigeria are a result of weak faith. The most serious problems today that call for concern are the unworthy habits of some parents who indulge in regrettable behaviours. Worst of all, most parents with no remorse at all, commit their mischiefs in the presence of their children. Examples of these mischiefs are.-Drinking alcohol, taking drugs, especially marijuana (Indian hemp) and cigarette smoking, as well as unwholesome utterances. Some parents now go to the extent of socializing shoulder to shoulder with their children. Therefore it is not surprising if a child that has this type of parent(s) grows up to be unfaithful and has social problems. These parents do not only spoil their children they also equally lead their neighbours' children astray. The sorry habit of drinking alcoholic beverages by parents is the major cause of their ineffectiveness in controlling and upbringing their children.

"*There was once a man, who was very wealthy and famous. He was well learned both in religious and secular knowledge. He had pretty wives who were blessed with many children. But this man had one flaw. He was an alcoholic. He could do anything when he got tipsy. One day he drove home from one of his drinking sprees, he sat down on a chair in front of his house to relax. Suddenly from his house came a beautiful girl who was a friend to his daughter. The girl bowed and greeted him, he responded fatherly. The girl walked away. She had not walked more than two hundred yards away when all of a sudden she was blocked by a slow-moving car. The car stopped and the driver asked her to get in the car. The girl immediately recognised the driver to be the father of her girlfriend. She declined his invitation, but he insisted that he was just trying to convey her home because it was getting dark. For this reason, the girl got in the car. As he was driving, he put his hand on her thigh. When the girl sensed what he was up to, she screamed. He immediately stopped the car and started scolding the girl, 'you are an uncivilized bush gift', he said. The girl got out of the car and ran home crying wildly*".

Now I want the reader to imagine the sorts of things this girl will think of this irresponsible father. When she narrates her story to her parents about this man, what would happen? What will become of the relationship between this girl and his daughter?

Moreover, when his daughter gets the wind of what occurred, what would be her reaction to her parents? This and similar mischiefs are the root causes of indiscipline and unfaithfulness in Nigeria. What will

be the fate of the children whose father parades the town at the night? The father is usually absent in the daytime, after working hours, he stays away from his family until late at night.
By the time he gets back, his children will be asleep, we all know these children are deprived of their fatherly love, and this will surely retard their moral and spiritual development. Therefore, it won't be surprised if these types of children grow up like their fathers or worse.

The aforementioned unbecoming behaviours of some parents surely mislead the young ones, and also this situation reveals the absence of faith in some parents. Any parent(s) who have solid faith in Allah and respect for their children will certainly shun these unwholesome behaviours. It is our responsibility as parents to make sure that our children are well-mannered. We should also teach those morals and the spirit of hard work. Manners and behaviours are best taught at an early age. Our children should be taught to respect their elders and neighbours, they should respect their guests too. In Hausa culture, it is considered a sign of good manners for a young boy/girl to greet his parents and relatives in the morning and the evening. Table manners and patience, perseverance are just a few of the many virtues parents should inculcate in their children.

Besides the parents, some of the leaders of various communities in Nigeria are also guilty of a lack of faith. According to our traditional values, leaders are accorded the highest prestige because of their wisdom, discipline, and fairness. But unfortunately, some of our leaders abuse their prestigious status by indulging in immoral activities e.g. drinking, extortion, romanticism and discrimination among their followers. These types of leaders should keep in mind that they are responsible for the general welfare of their followers, and they are accountable to Allah for their tenure in office. These wrongdoings of our leaders surely are a major cause of indiscipline in Nigeria. There is a true story about a Chief and his subject. The events in the story occurred during the tax collection period. This short story will help the reader to grasp the extent of the atrocities committed by some of our leaders against their subjects to satisfy their selfish interests.

"E*very year just after the period of harvesting the seasonal crops, it was time for tax collection. The very year in which this event took place wasn't a good year for farmers who accidentally constitute more than three-quarters of the population of the subjects ruled by this chief. But as usual, the chief went ahead with his normal business of tax collection. Among the subjects was one farmer, who had four adult sons, unfortunately, this poor farmer had very many family problems. Moreover, the year hadn't been any good for him, so he was late in paying his tax. One afternoon, the chief went to collect the tax money from the farmer, and he found him working hard together with his sons on the farm. The chief demanded the tax money, and the farmer asked for another extension of the deadline. Suddenly, without any diplomatic dialogue, the chief absurdly slapped this poor farmer on the face twice in the presence of his four sons. The chief also viciously scolded the poor farmer*".

The oppression of people by some of our leaders as

well as the callous relationship between our leaders and the rest of us (the ruled) isn't conducive to fostering a just, disciplined and egalitarian society. We must all desist from our selfishness to enrich our faith and develop a disciplined society. Leaders should always live exemplary lives, they should be patient, humble in dealing with their subjects, self-disciplined, fair and most of all they should be faithful. For our leaders to be unanimously accepted, obeyed and respected they should possess the above-mentioned qualities, but we must also assist our leaders to be effective by seeing to it that every one of us possesses the same above-outlined qualities. Our religious leaders are very much responsible for the inculcation of discipline in our young ones as well as the society if large. But a good number of them, unfortunately, are retrogressive in fostering morality and general discipline in our society.

Numerous examples are bound to elaborate on the depth and complexity of the misdemeanour committed by these Religious leaders. Some of these leaders preach Religion according to their selfish interests. They can be identified by their tendencies to incite one group of people against another, or unjustifiably stir a group of people against the legally constituted authority. They are the *do-as-I-say-not-as-I-do* types. They are excellent in paying lip service to religion but fall short of practicing what religion advocates. This is surely the worst type of unfaithfulness. A model Religious leader is self-disciplined, and a living example of what he professes to his disciples.

Looking at another corner of our society, we will see that the well-to-do among us are also partly responsible for the lack of morals and discipline in our society. This consists of petty traders, merchants, contractors and modern international businessmen and women.

Hoarders of essential commodities abound among these people. It is unfaithful for any Muslim to hoard essential commodities. In Islam, the appropriate penalty that awaits any person who fails to desist from this criminal act is eternal life in HELL in the hereafter. In addition to hoarding, our businessmen and women indulge in pretense and deception to amass wealth. So it is obvious that these people aren't disciplined. They are unfit to be models for others to emulate. There is a Hausa adage that says "*fadin gaskiya yafi mugunyar salla*" Literally, it means telling the truth is more honourable than a shabby prayer. By implication, this means that the little money made honestly is far worthier than the millions amassed through hoarding and deception.

Moreover, we should all know that deception, hoarding, or any other personal efforts don't make people rich. Richness is from Allah. If fate has it that one is going to be rich, surely one will become rich. So one should make one's money honestly. Therefore to foster morality and discipline in our society, business people should be honest, cease hoarding and sell their articles of trade at normal prices.

We will now turn our eyes towards the Civil and the Public servants of all ranks and file. This includes

Judges, police, army, teachers, doctors, commissioners, ministers, governors and also the Head of State as well as a host of others. Judges are supposedly well-learned people, and full of wisdom.

Therefore they are charged with the responsibility of maintaining justice and protecting the right of every citizen. Justice here is meant for the establishment of an impartial system of defending and protecting every citizen. It is also pertinent to the legal profession for a judge to be fearful of his God and to discharge cases impartially. No judge should be tempted with bribery or allowed to be blackmailed at the expense of an innocent citizen.

It is only the Judge who can resist the above weaknesses that is capable of showing examples of discipline and dedication.

The situation in Nigeria is such that the powerful and the wealthy have tamed our courts and their Judges. They get people convicted or acquitted as they wish. In short, they monopolise and guide the course of proceedings. These pressure groups of people or their associates can commit murder and easily get away with it. The corruption of our legal system is largely due to the practice of legal administrators. After enacting a law, they are usually the first to bend that law to suit their interests. The following narration will illuminate the above point.

"*In a faraway land there was once a judge, he had the reputation of being honest and incorruptible. Moreover, he had a knack for handling cases efficiently and judiciously. One day, a case of deceit involving two people, one rich and the other poor. In this case, it was the rich man who cheated the poor. After listening to them, it became apparent to the judge that the rich man cheated the poor. The judge instantly told the rich man that it was wrong of him to have cheated the poor man.*

Therefore, he ordered the case to be adjourned, until the following week, when he will pronounce the judgment. After the case was adjourned, the rich man proceeded to lobby for a favour from his connections within the Ministry of Justice, Being very connected, he got his favour, and the judge was sent a letter from the Ministry advising him to either dismiss the case or try it in favour of the rich man. Moreover, he was even sent for, he went to the Ministry where he was further reminded that the case before him was a special case to be treated with caution and according to the guidelines from the Ministry".

In this context, how could this judge perform his duty efficiently and judiciously?
It is obvious that if this judge decided to try this case impartially, he risk losing his job, and to do the contrary will cost him his good reputation. These unwanted situations in our courts are a major cause of indiscipline in Nigeria. To uphold the dignity of our legal systems, these situations and their architects must be flushed out of the profession entirely, therefore, this is the task before our legal system.

The police force in Nigeria are also corrupt, in some situation, their presence makes no difference whatsoever. The bad eggs among them aid smugglers and hoarders in committing vicious crimes against the many defenseless Nigerians. The greedy policemen have been reduced to mere bodyguards of the rich, if you can tip three to five Naira to a policeman, you can get away with any horrible crime. The only law-abiding citizens in Nigeria are the lower class. The Nigeria Police Force has a great task ahead of it. It must screen its force carefully and filter out the unfit members to restore discipline in the force. This will enable the masses of Nigeria to have confidence in the Police Force, but as of now, the public confidence in the force is at its lowest ebb.

Teachers in public schools lack dedication. They hold their jobs with contempt. Their performance does not compensate for the huge amount of money spent on education. Teachers in our schools should remember that they have taken the oath of office to serve their country, therefore, anything short of this is a breach of oath and they can be held accountable. Moreover, the duty of teachers is more than classroom teaching, they should also teach moral character and general discipline to their children/students. They should teach them acceptable social manners and behaviours such as; mode of dressing, participation in public activities, mode of speech especially public speaking morals etc. Therefore teachers must be of high moral standard. This attitude will ensure the revitalization of indiscipline in our society.

Categories of public and civil servants are numerous and different. So are their responsibilities.
But despite these differences, they have one responsibility In common. They should all be dedicated to their work, they should discharge their responsibilities to the best of their abilities and they should also fear God. It is unethical for a public civil

servant to siphon public funds for his/her selfish ends. Such ill-gotten funds will surely be accounted for either here or in the hereafter, where the guilty has to pay back for his misdeeds in one's good deeds. Similarly, high-ranking officials should know that they are accountable to Allah. Surely, Allah will ask them to account for the responsibilities accorded them in this world. Therefore, officials should make sure that all the rank and file under their leadership discharge their duties with a great sense of probity and efficiency. Allah says that surely on the Day of Judgment He will recover for the poor and the weak what has been confiscated from them by the powerful in this world.

It is up to us to be on good terms with our Lord God. For He is the best judge of all actions, and he alone knows best what we are up to. Those among us who repent their sins and decide to play their roles in this terminal world according to the rules and regulations of Allah will surely meet with the blessings of Allah. And on the other hand, those who go astray living purposely for the present world will surely meet with the wrath of Allah. May we all meet with the blessings of Almighty Allah, Amen.

A person who has no clean heart has an incurable disease, no matter what material things or power he has in his possession, the surest way for one to be free of this disease is, to be honest, hardworking and impartial in dealing with others. In short, one should be disciplined. Moreover, one should not resent ones' self for failures, or weakness.
One should be proud of oneself. Health, food, and a

humble shelter are good enough for a decent living. May Allah guide us on the right path. Amen.

CHAPTER THREE

MODESTY MAKES A PERSON

Nigeria is a plural society. It has different tribes with various cultures consequently their systems of character training and discipline remarkably vary. For example, in Islam, there are different modes of character training and discipline. A Muslim who practices/uses these methods is easily discerned from one who does not.

This is also true of our traditional heritage. What is considered a traditional etiquette in a Hausa community, e.g. talking to an older person with a low tone, may not be so in other cultures. For example, in some Yoruba communities, it is acceptable for a FIANCEE to be pregnant before she weds her FIANCE, this also proves that she is fertile. But in the Hausa community, this is unlawful. A bride can only give birth at least five months after the marriage, for the baby to be considered legitimate.

Humility is a prerequisite to character training and general discipline in the Hausa community, Prophet Muhammad (peace be upon him) said "an *immodest person is unreliable. Hence he/she shouldn't be obliged any responsibility*". Moreover, it is emphatically said that humility is essential to faith. It is when one can cultivate humility that one can have and cherish faith. All these virtues are necessary for character training, which is socializing a person or persons to learn and, accept and also adopt the given community.

What is Humility? Humility is the ability to keep away from any form of indiscipline, economic or social, moreover, it is also the courage to be generally modest, it is said that charity begins at home, and it is the responsibility of every household to fight against indiscipline. This should begin with the inculcation of attitudes of humility. The head of the family should be a humble person. This will set an example for the other members of the family to emulate. It is scandalous for a household head to engage in irresponsible pursuits. Nowadays, unfortunately, it has become a vogue for one to keep a chain of girlfriends and be popular at beer-parlous. A person who does not indulge in these activities is an anti-social bushman. Today, many married men frequent brothers who patronize these whore houses.
Some Nigerians now in the name of being highly social, allow their wives to visit neighbouring cities and even countries to spend the weekends while they stay back home to drink and commit adultery.

According to Islam, these acts are sinful, therefore, unlawful for a Muslim.

The next task for the members of the household to accomplish particularly the husband and the wife/wives is to put a full stop to seemingly incessant household quarrels. Husband and wife should not quarrel in the presence of their children, nor should they fight. All arising matters should be settled humbly and democratically, and when appropriate in the presence of their children.

Excessive permissiveness and lack of firmness and flexibility in dealing with the young ones spoil them completely. Children should be disciplined, parents should always check their attitudes and behaviour to make sure they don't expose their children to vices such as an extravagance, arrogance, sheer cruelty or wickedness etc. For all these are forbidden by Allah. A humble and disciple household head shouldn't be extravagant with his savings/earnings so as not to give his children a false belief that affluence is the most important of all things he should be thrifty. The guiding principle for a household/family is to be a living example for their children and others to imitate. When a father forbids his son from smoking, he too should not smoke.

In matrimonial cases, discipline and modesty are priceless items. Before marriage was a peaceful, memorable, non-commercial uniting of different families. A man cannot wed a girl until her family background is ascertained and approved, her character is also vital, she has to be of sound moral character and well disciplined. But today, marriages (most) of them are just commercial ventures. The parents of the girl are only looking for the highest bidder to give their daughter to, for marriage. A man can be very virtuous but will be denied a girl's hand in marriage if he is poor. Virtue and principles are no longer assets for getting married. Just have Naira, no matter how it is always certain you can get a girl to marry from any family of one's choice. In this situation, how do we expect to have disciplined and humbly children? The same goes for the girls. For a girl to be popular and have a parade of suitors from which to select, she has to be from a wealthy family. This is contrary to Islamic marriage arrangements and doesn't teach discipline and humility.

Teachers of both religion and secular education have a role to play in teaching our children. A few years back and even now, though to a lesser degree, teachers you respected. Teachers were ideal models, well disciplined, behaved, modest, industrious and virtuous. Now things have changed for the worst. Some of our religious leaders/teachers have chosen to be puppets or stooges for the rich and the powerful. Go to any wealthy man's house, you are sure to find our Mallams squatting by the door all day long to get a naira or two from the Alhaji. In the process, they backbite and tell lies or jokes just to please Alhaji into throwing out some money to them. Some can even be seen at mixed political party meetings, launchings or rallies.

Gosh! what a terrible reversal of things. It is unfortunate that the government now is calling these teachers to preach to the public about the spirit of

War against Indiscipline. Are they disciplined themselves to start with? The late famous Narambada (A famous Hausa singer) has this to say about these

- A knowledgeable person who refuses to put his knowledge to good use is doomed.
- He should forever go astray.
- There are many of such amidst us.
- They shall never
- Realise a thing in their lives.

Let us turn our eyes toward the teachers of Western education.

In the early days, students worked hard to copy their teachers.
A teacher was a living example of a self-actualized person. Disciplined in every aspect of life, respected and loved. Those teachers treated their students as their children, their word was DISCIPLINE, character training and handwork are primary objectives in the education of their students. In recent years, a good number of teachers are first in breaking the school rules. What goes on in our schools is quite alarming. This unfortunate situation can be blamed on the Ministry of Education in the country for some reasons. Viz.

The Proliferation of Schools

The number of schools established was just incredible the ratio of teachers/students was miserably disproportionate. The number of students in our schools is too much for the teachers to control. For this reason, the students take to different mischiefs. Moreover, women's education in some communities in Nigeria is viewed with contempt, even the government puts less emphasis on women's education. More disappointing is the ***"day schools"*** for girls. These schools lack an effective link between them and the individual homes of these students that will monitor the activities that take place when these students set out to go to school and also when coming back from school. Consequently, the wicked people among us take advantage of these innocent young girls luring them into immoral activities. The implications of this are reaching and numerous.

It can lead to unwanted pregnancies, prostitution, drop-outs, venereal disease and other acts of indiscipline. In the Northern part of Nigeria, the ancient method of checking the above situation was strict surveillance of the girl's movements. She has to account for every absence, or errand she has undertaken, she also remains in this condition until she is married to a decent, disciplined and hardworking man.

We Nigerians must make sure that our young girls conduct themselves according to the laid down principles. For example, in the Northern part of Nigeria, Muslim girls must behave per the ethics of the Islamic religion. The same religious ethics should be the Guiding principles of women's education and all their interactions with male members of society. The Ministry of education has to protect these innocent girls. Their movements to and from schools should be monitored by the authority to ensure discipline within and outside the school. It is the negligence of this responsibility that is causing the present in-disciplinary behaviour in our schools. We shouldn't allow our schools to turn into match-making centres, for none of us would like to have his daughter led astray in the name of attending school to seek knowledge.

Similarly, our leaders must also protect themselves from acts that disgrace them and what they stand for. They should be just and fair and possess a high moral character so that they can protect their public image. Our leaders should be able to communicate effectively with their people.

And they should be fair and just in their daily dealings with people, they should be wary of oppression, their people should not grumble about unfair treatment, and all should be treated equally. When we talk of lack of character, indiscipline, traitor ship, etc., most people will shift the blame onto our leaders and the elite among us. The elites are the public servants and the well-to-do. This is squarely true because these people are assigned to the task of managing society. They should make sure that every member of society is adequately protected and well catered for.

At this age, Nigerians shouldn't allow themselves to be fooled by any con man. The appearance of any kind whether physical or material shouldn't deceive us. Many a time we have been fooled and deceived by politicians and some spiritual leaders, who tell us to do one thing while they do another. It is our responsibility to know our rights and obligations to our country. It is disappointing to see in Nigeria that highly placed civil servants are notorious for committing in-disciplinary acts, they come late to work, leave before the right time, receive kickbacks and defraud the government of millions of Naira annually. For example, government vehicles and their drivers work twenty-four hours a day, they are always seen going on different errands in the town after working hours. They are used to convey the Bosses' mistresses or to go shopping for them.

All the problems enumerated in the preceding paragraphs are mainly caused by a lack of sense of responsibility, accountability and dedication. But it is quite obvious that whenever people lack modesty, good character and general discipline, they will certainly fall prey to the aforementioned vices and many more. We all need to re-examine ourselves, we should know our places in our community and look forward to knowing how much we can contribute to our community. It is time we all purify our hearts and approach our responsibilities with disciplined attitudes.

Street begging, house to house and office to office begging and loafing should be discouraged, people should be enlightened and encouraged to see the evils of begging and dependency. But many people now make a second living on this, there is even a new breed of beggars, who ride motorbikes or bicycles going from one place to another asking for money or favours from their acquaintances. If one fails to oblige to their request, one is proclaimed a miser and the slander will be spread throughout the neighbourhood. In Nigerian Communities, usually loafing is the begging of a career in robbery or pimping. The unsuccessful imps resort to homosexuality, a very lucrative career in Nigeria. Oh! God. There is an urgent need to cast off laziness in Nigeria. And also to de-emphasize the attitude of getting things for nothing. Spirit of hand work and pride in one's earnings should be instilled in our hearts. The Nigerian Government should embark on massive adult education, the young ones should be sent to schools and the adult should attend adult literacy, classes. Moreover, the elites of this country should cease their habit of taking advantage of the ignorance of the majority, they must teach this majority the right things. They should help protect their interest not just rip it off.

The most immediate task ahead of us now, especially our elites is to shun materialism. Nigerians should be humble and self-controlled, we should all realise a kobo honestly earned is worth more than a hundred Naira ill-gotten, for Allah is ever pleased with the honest.

May Allah show us and guide us to the right path and may we never go astray, let us pray to Allah to make us humble enough to respect and abide by his commands and be sufficiently vigorous to keep away from his prohibitions, Amen.

CHAPTER FOUR

PATIENCE PAYS

Patience is something that should be exercised by every well-meaning individual, especially at a time of need, loss or want.

An individual can be described as a patient when he or she at a time of strain and stress, regulates himself/herself to absorb them as if they were a normal course of living. A patient person is constantly worry-free. No doubt patience is an important element needed for any leadership quality.
The importance of exercising patience is very crucial. Prophet Muhammad (peace be upon him) repeatedly called Muslims to be patient. "Abu Huraira (R.A) a leading Islamic Scholar reported that 'once a man called on the prophet and asked him (the prophet) to tell him the most beneficial work (among the tenets of Islam) he could do for himself, the Prophet said to the man 'BE PATIENT' On insistence, the prophet replied again that he should not be annoyed rather he

should be patient over whatever situation he finds himself". This, therefore, explains the importance of being patient in the course of one's life.

The opposite of patience is impatience, whose attributes are always negative, they include indiscipline, greed, misdemeanour avarice and a host of others, and whose presence in an individual renders him self-centered, perturbed and unfulfilled, which always puts one in a botched situation.
Perhaps guardians or those who are entrusted with the upbringing of little ones, a high degree of patience is expected of them. Children are by nature imitative, they are prone to blind imitation and hero worship, which means children copy whatever they see adults do whether good or bad for they are in no position to distinguish between the two. Therefore the need to be scrupulously careful and patient in dealing with them cannot be over-emphasized.

It is often found that teachers with a hot temper do not make good teachers because all the time the children are tensed for fear of the whip. In such an atmosphere, children learn little or none. To impart meaningful skills and ideas to the children, a teacher needs to be persuasive, preserving, patient and kind.

Our undoing impatience has cut across sectorial bounds both social and domestic, this bane of our society has especially eaten deep in our traditional institutions who are supposed to be the custodians of our tradition, culture and values. The sycophants most of whom are the architects of indiscipline, rumour mongers, and mischief makers are part and parcel of these otherwise noble institutions. The desire to become rich or 'succeed' at jet-speed has become a valuating ambition to many Nigerian at the expense of hard work and honesty. A situation where contracts and inflated goods are hoarded, traders milk the customers, and policemen rob citizens, only brings about anarchy. One other disturbing situation is that even some of our religious leaders and moral instructors are not untainted. Cases abound where Clergy/Priest/Mallam rapes, dupes or thieves, and corruption of the highest order are said to exist in these institutions.

The laxity of our elders and the lassie-fair attitude of the parents in the upbringing of their children contributed massively to the falling standard of education. It has now become normal for parents to rain abuse or 'mute' teachers for meeting out the lightest punishment to their children (for misbehaviour, bullying and countless offences common in children). Sometimes such teachers end up in court, for upholding the ethics of their profession what a great departure from the past when teachers were regarded with reverence. While it is true that children are to be treated with the utmost care, love and affection, a certain amount of punishment is desirable to mould good characters in them. The parlance "spare the rod and spoil the child" should be constantly remembered by the parents.

The teaching profession is not completely exonerated for the falling standard of education. It has its share of the blame. Amongst the teachers themselves, indiscipline of intolerable level is manifested. Oftentimes, teachers are found poorly clad, poorly educated morally bankrupt, then how for goodness sake do you expect any meaningful learning to take place in such atmosphere?

Whatever ones vacation or trade, the need to be honest and upright ensures the success of such ventures, leaders who are neck and daunt make for good leadership, they are powerful and respected, whereas the rulers are dishonest and selfish ones is characterized by repression bankruptcy and decadence.

In those days when morality was our society's bedrock, respect for elders and constituted authorities had pride of place, communalism and wholesome human relatives were exemplified. We had a philosophy of live and let live and we were our brother's keepers; of course, the general life then was pleasurable.

The chaotic as well as disorder less nature of a Nigerian is manifested when it comes to Joining the queues at public, places, i.e. in Banks, Hospitals, Airports, Motor parks, Stadia and a host of other public-oriented places. He likes to jump or shunt queues, average Nigerian is selfish, impatient, stubborn, self-seeking and egotistic. It is only in Nigeria that tickets are Okayed at the airports for intending travelers for instance triple the available number of seats, whereas a Nigerian away from 'homes' is sober, peace loving and law abiding. What a paradox?

CHAPTER FIVE

THE HONEST IS LOVE BY ALL

As the popular adage goes "an *honest person is loved by all*" especially when the person in question is a juvenile. This is, however, not an attribute restricted to the youth alone. Honest adults too could be acknowledged with such remarks. It follows that children of an honest and upright person grow up to be associated with similar virtues. An ideal father is decent and modest all the time.

To be an ideal house-holder encompasses a thorough knowledge of monitoring every activity within the home. This is intended to sanction any unpleasant development. Children should be restrained from engaging in mischievous peer groups that might mislead them. Children should be guided, be honest coupled with moral or religious training. Invariably it is good to train children to be courteous. They should also be trained to be courteous to visitors and learn to respect elders. 'It is pertinent also that children must learn to respect their mothers and their relatives.

The above conditions could be missing where the father alienates himself from the company of his children at home and engages in excess drunkenness. This father could be seen as a stranger in his own house, he is also shirking his responsibilities.

There could still be people who are considered honest from amongst the learned (religious intellectuals/Mallams). An honest preacher/Mallam is blunt and truthful no matter whose ox is god. This is important because his disciples are likely to go by his examples. It is the height of dishonesty and almost irreligious for a preacher to engage in a beggary and insatiable quest for material possessions. A preacher should be a righteous and disciplined person, he should also abstain from an undue search for material wealth. This does not prevent the preachers from engaging in legitimate trade or any enterprise that could fetch income. Provided the business is lawful and does not in any way subject his personality to ridicule.

Some preachers could also violate state laws, by engaging in incestuous, slanderous, or libelous propaganda to tarnish the image of some innocent persons. This is an abuse of intellectual privilege and subsequently a dishonest act.

The prophet Muhammad (peace be upon him) in his infinite wisdom once said that "the learned are the inheritors of the prophet" In essence, preachers are supposed to promote and safeguard the noble teaching of the prophet. In the true spirit of the prophet's injunction on the learned people, preachers should learn to the best of their ability how to be disciplined in the prophet's way. It is a well-known fact that Prophet Muhammad (peace be upon him) was a peacemaker.

There are also honest people from among the traditional rulers. An honest traditional ruler ensures social justice, equality of men and regard for human dignity. It is a pity not that most of our traditional rulers are more interested in revenue collection than the promotion of the welfare of their people.
If an opinion poll were to be conducted on the payment of poll and cattle tax, it will be discovered that the citizens don't intend to evade tax, but were only disturbed and harassed by the traditional rulers in the process of collecting the revenue. Just like the already mentioned case of a traditional ruler who took the law into his own hands by assaulting/slapping a taxpayer who was pleading for an extension of time for payment. Our citizens suffer untold hardship at the hands of traditional rulers through the process of revenue collection and other governmental services that require the active involvement of traditional rulers in mobilizing their subjects.

There remains a crop of charismatic traditional rulers whose subjects are willing to make any sacrifice on their behalf. A closer examination of this type of chief would reveal that he is generous and considerate towards his people. This country is searching for such leaders at the moment who would provide the leader in our March towards a disciplined society for others to follow.

Honest businessmen are those who work towards the commercial advancement of their people through the sale of essential commodities to the public at a government-controlled price. It is un-Islamic for any businessman to hoard any commodity.

This is only an attribute of inhumanity and the absence of faith. It does not pay to acquire riches through the exploitation of your fellow men and women. Traders are hereby reminded of enemies which will inevitably catch up with them. The activities of hoarders are vicious and numerous. If our people do not expose the hoarders, what will eventually result in this country? Disasters and woes normally await such a country.

Traders should note that when any disaster befalls this country they have no other country but Nigeria. If they think otherwise, they must be living in a fool's paradise. Wealth could naturally come through sustained hard work and good enterprise and not hurriedly through the sale of commodities at sky-rocketed prices. Posterity will judge these unpatriotic traders and emesis will not spare anyone.
Honest people could be found in any section of the public service, so are redundant and inefficient workers.

The services of our electronic media, i.e. Radio and Television leave much to be desired after almost a decade of their existence, even though some of their programs are interesting and commendable, others

are counter-productive as well as unsuitable for our environment. One could say with an air of certainty that, Radio and Television have contributed immensely through the electronic media that tribal chauvinism and the adoption of foreign cultures were propagated to the detriment of the more unspoiled indigenous culture of our people.
Most Radio stations were used by governments in power to either exaggerate or tell blunt lies to favour the governments.

The last discredited Civilian Administration witnessed a spate of interference in broadcasting by the powers that be. An absolute dictatorship and lack of freedom of expression existed then, while politicians get access to Radio and Television to tell the most horrible incredible lies to the audience, public opinion was, however, muzzled. The unpatriotic way in which our Television stations were being used gave a more devastating blow to democracy. It was clear then that the management of our Television stations was most unpatriotic in the sense that they betrayed the majority of this country only to serve a few individuals, knowing fully well that nemesis would eventually catch up with them.

Children and the rest members of the family in the cities are indoctrinated to appreciate foreign cultures through imported films, our youths almost worship foreign films, especially American, Chinese and Indian movies. This is without a corresponding enthusiasm for our local musicians who are often discarded by our youth. It is criminal for our Television stations to promote obscenity through foreign films that vividly depict acts of sophisticated crimes.

Others like boxing and wrestling mainly depict violence and brutality. Surprising enough, our traditional family set-up and child-rearing have been deserted for a foreign one. Parents, however, could only frown when they notice some antisocial behaviour in their children, not knowing that foreign films are the tool causes of such developments. Children at their tender age may fail to see the reason why parents should restrain them when Television stars mainly adults were seen doing similar things on the screens.

Acts of disrespect to parents could be seen on our screens in episodes where children disagree vehemently with their parents. The China's 'KUNG FU' and the American 'ELECTRIC BOOGALOOS' dance are the major preoccupations of our youth. Thus, traditional dances and 'moonlight plays' by our youths have been relegated to the background. Only the rural youths are left out in the de-culture process of the effects of Television.

Traditional ethics and values are the main sources of discipline. Any departure from our traditional values could only lead to indiscipline and, chaos and confusion.

Government should take bold steps now to review our cultural heritage and substitute foreign films with locally made films. To achieve this, the government has to emulate the successful struggles and revolutions of some developed countries that succeeded in evolving a just and disciplined society.

This country has a reserve of potential in all spheres of human endeavour, especially in the field of poetry and music. Their songs could inspire orderly conduct and the promotion of a decent society.

Hail! Our past leaders who were the custodians of our traditions, without their unyielding posture towards foreign taste, could have by now forgotten most of our traditional dresses like the Gown. We are appreciative that our traditional attire was not phased out. Till now, one is viewed with respect all over the world when he dresses in our traditional outfit. If we had not lost our traditional sense of values, ours would have been a better society worthy of emulation by others.

Lest I forget, our cinema houses contributed in no small measure to our present predicament in terms of inspiring indiscipline in our people. What is the rationale for our governments allowing the screening of obscenities, crime and violence in our cinema houses? Though viewed mildly by some people, could unfold a danger.

CHAPTER SIX

SUGGESTIONS FOR IMPROVEMENT

Although this book emphasizes more the sociocultural arrangements of moral standards and general discipline of the Muslims, the suggestions that will follow will be general in the scope of including all parts of the country. This general approach aims to forge sociocultural unity among all the tribes in Nigeria.

The suggestions, if patriotically utilised by Nigerians, will go a long way in improving our morality and ensuring general discipline in society.

The suggestions consist of sociocultural aspects that require some rectifications to achieve considerable improvements in moral standards and general discipline.

THE IDEAL MORALS AND DISCIPLINE THAT SHOULD BE TAUGHT

- **Leadership by Example:** Discipline can only succeed if our leaders show the masses that they are disciplined in their day-to-day affairs. They have to be seen, to be honest, here we have to categorise some aspects of leadership. We have religious leaders; traditional rulers or Emirs, and those who lead simply because they are endowed with material wealth.

- **Corruption and Gratification:** So long as the government remains dismal in its efforts to fight the evils of corruption and gratification, the efforts to achieve a disciplined society will be fruitless. It is an enormous task on the part of the government to eradicate these two evils that bedevil this country as those who are entrusted with enforcing law and order are allegedly the culprits.

- **Favoritism (godfather):** is the act of giving an appointment or post to somebody or mere favour simply because, he or she is related to somebody, or entirely on another ground. Contracts are given to those with connections and terms of fulfilling the contracts are thrown to the dogs. This is one place where the government must stand on its feet. Can government win against these people?

- **Unqualified persons (Manpower Mismanagement):** is one area, where a person who does not qualify for a job, is given that job to do. For example, a teacher may be employed as an Administrative Officer, or an Engineer may be assigned purely administrative tasks. This doesn't augur well for any Organisation.

- **Punishment**: It is only by way of punishing the guilty person by making an example of him that you get a disciplined society. For Nigeria, a stage has been reached whereby it is only the common man who suffers as far as breaking the law is concerned. Those who are wealthy could afford to buy their way out when an offence or crime is committed. This is the crux of the problem in Nigeria. Laws of the land are broken with impunity. It is of paramount importance, that anybody who commits a crime should be punished according to the dictates of the law.

- **Unemployment**: In matters of unemployment, the government must find gainful employment for its people. It is foolhardy to expect somebody who has no work to do, to listen to the various campaigns against indiscipline.

- **Procurement of Food and Essential Commodities** It is difficult for the war against indiscipline to succeed when the public is fighting another war, viz war against scarcity of food and consumer items, especially when they see their leaders giving parties as if there is no scarcity around.

- **Nation Building:** The people of this country have multifarious problems that have to do with nation-building. The majority of our people are self-centred, more interested in themselves than in the nation, generally. This has to do with leadership. We have leaders who cherish 'tribalism' and differences in 'Religion'. As far as trading is concerned you find people of various persuasions, religions, and differences conducting their affairs so that they could obtain material wealth. Hausa, Igbo and Yoruba conduct their day-to-day affairs without any hitch. It is now apparent and unfortunate that some people are using religion and tribal excuses to divide the people of this country.

  In the end, you find that it is the poor man who suffers and the ***detriment*** of the progress of the country; as long as people are left to continue with this type of exploitation and nothing is done to check them this country can never be united.

- **Mass Enlightenment (Publicity):** The tendency of leaving people in the dark, without necessarily informing them of anything beforehand, is one of the nagging problems facing this country. Here I do not mean that the government does not take the necessary steps to explain, but what I mean is that those who understand government and its mechanics are purely the educated, and even the educated, the elite. Any government programme meant for the people can only succeed if people are knowledgeable and are aware of what is happening, it is a difficult task to impart information to someone illiterate without encountering many problems, there is what we can rightly call the information gap. Government programmes are not much published so that the general public may know what the government is up to. Any government programme beneficial to the public can only be useful if the people understand it and appreciate its significance. This is a difficult task on its own.

- **Religious Teachers:** One of the reasons why our society has sunk so deep into indiscipline is the way religious and moral teachings are thrown to the dogs. It is a task of immense importance that the government pay more attention to this. We are a living witness of what has happened in Kano the ***MAITATSINE'S uprising***, here are people who had taken the law into their hands. It is only when the damage was done, that haphazard measures were taken to avert a recurrence. Some religious teachers are to be blamed for the lack of discipline in society. Most of them cherish and engage in verbal tirades among themselves. It is important here to point out the urgent need for a religious body that will oversee the activities of religious leaders, and preachers in every nook and corner of this country.

- **Paying More Attention to Religion:** We have to embrace religious teachings as vehicles for attaining a disciplined society. Religion, be it Islam, or Christianity, every of them, has ways to lead its adherents to a better lifestyle. People in this country believe in the tenets of their religions, and they want to do nothing that will transgress on them.

- **Alcoholism:** It is of paramount importance that places of drinking are reduced, especially in places or, states, which have a Moslem majority. Addictive drugs should be banned especially in schools. It is now obvious that violent demonstrations are after the effect of excessive student drinking sprees. If at all, the government should do something to see to the reduction in the number of drinking parlous, then something positive is being achieved. There are a lot of people who are against the idea of burning some beer houses. These types of people are those who have reached a point of no return in this preoccupation. Alcohol is evil in its totality, it is harmful to the body. It is in short, toxic. May God show us the right path, Amen.

- **Brothers:** Nobody still wants to see brothers springing up in his town or village. Nobody will want to see his daughter turn into a prostitute or a free woman. No good person can condone prostitution where he lives. Why are there people, unfortunately, highly placed condoning this institution? Every government must see that this institution is abolished once and for all.

- **Media Houses:** Media Houses have played a role in seeing to the disunity of the masses of this nation who are known to be disciplined with commendable ways of life. Nobody has given them this opportunity except that they were not opportune to live in this given situation that now is the talk of the day. This is so because, most of them are displeased with the Whiteman and anybody who dares to coax them into refusing, except the state government, the ways of life left by the Whiteman, will not easily succeed. It is a shame to see a good friend who could perform well and then only performs below expectations. It is incumbent upon the media houses to see to it, that the general public is enlightened and informed of the day-to-day happenings in their surroundings. It is also vital for them to dish out correct information which will not mislead the public.

Media houses in any given society, have always a vital role to play in the progress and wellbeing of the community in which they are heated. It will be unbecoming and will not serve us any good to allow phonographic films imported into our country. More so, films that portray thefts or violence. Before allowing such films to flood the country they have to be censored. Those that are found to be unfit should be destroyed.

- **Ostentation:** This adage "*Danhakinda ka rena shine ke tsone ma ido*" can easily be translated thus 'You should not despise anything that you think is harmless' because it might injure you in the long run. We should try as much as possible to shy away from Nigerians. Where do we go from here? With this form of indoctrination, it is difficult to find a boy or a girl invested in the mode of dresses obtained in his locality. It is gross indiscipline and un-Islamic to see a girl improperly dressed. Any right-thinking person will castigate the way she dressed. In a Hausa society, a boy who dresses up in the Western way will receive verbal condemnation. We pray to God that we should see the path of truth and be able to follow it, see the path of untruth and refuse to succumb to it. We pray to God in to help us to have a disciplined society, to obey all rightful instructions to the way of an ideal society now and hereafter.

ABOUT THE AUTHOR

Hadi Abdullahi Alkanci, the famous writer of Hausa Drama, was born on January 1, 1957, and died in 2009 in the Alkanci area of Sokoto. He studied at Kofar Marke Nizzamiyya school (now Alhaji Alhaji Model Primary School, Sokoto). In 1973 he went to Sultan Abubakar College Sokoto, where he graduated as a Grade II Teacher in 1977. He worked in the Education Department of Sokoto Local Government and taught at Army Children School Sokoto from 1977-78. He then went to Staff Training Center (now College of Administration, Sokoto) where he did a certificate in Translation in 1978-79. He worked at Rima Radio Sokoto and then he retired and started a business, at this time he joined N.T.A Lagos, where he presented a program called "WAZOBIA" and he also worked as a journalist from 1981- 82. He became one of the main directors of ALKANCI ENTERPRISE. At this time, he had the opportunity to visit many countries around the world. In 1986, he left the business and returned to focus on writing and journalism. Mr Hadi Alkanci has presented various papers at conferences of writers and literature in different universities outside of this country and he was a famous Hausa dramatist. In 1981, his first book titled "Soyayya tafi Kudi" was published by the Ministry of Foreign Affairs. He has written several books. After that, he wrote many books that were not been published yet. He is a member of ANA and contributed a lot to the development of Hausa literature, especially in the Sokoto state. Thus, everyone who knows him, distinguishes him as a writer.

www.ingramcontent.com/pod-product-compliance
Lightning Source LLC
LaVergne TN
LVHW050345160826
845677LV00014B/3807
* 9 7 9 8 3 5 3 4 5 3 2 6 0 *